WORLD TRAVELER

HOLY LAND

GALLERY BOOKS
An Imprint of W. H. Smith Publishers Inc.
112 Madison Avenue
New York City 10016

This edition first published in U.S.
in 1990 by Gallery Books,
an imprint of W.H. Smith Publishers, Inc.
112 Madison Avenue, New York, New York 10016

ISBN 0-8317-0255-9

Printed and bound in Spain

For rights information about the photographs in
this book please contact:

The Image Bank
111 Fifth Avenue, New York, NY 10003

Producer: Solomon M. Skolnick
Writer: Lee Server
Design Concept: Lesley Ehlers
Designer: Ann-Louise Lipman
Editor: Sara Colacurto
Production: Valerie Zars
Photo Researcher: Edward Douglas
Assistant Photo Researcher: Robert V. Hale
Editorial Assistant: Carol Raguso

Title page: Beyond the Dead Sea, the
sun rises over the Holy Land. No region
in history has played a more profound
and long-lasting role in human events.
Opposite: The walled city of ancient
Jerusalem was virtually impregnable
except for a series of narrow, guarded
gateways. The now-sealed Golden Gate
is on the east side of the Old City.

A detailed model of old Jerusalem shows the Second Jewish Temple, which was destroyed by the Romans around 70 A.D. and never rebuilt. *Opposite:* Jerusalem, Israel, is sometimes called the City of Gold, and was once considered the center of the world. Nearly 5,000 years old, it is one of the oldest continuously inhabited communities in the history of civilization.

The golden Dome of the Rock in Jerusalem is the 1,300-year-old Muslim shrine protecting the sacred rock where King David had his Altar of the Lord. The Dome of the Rock is also the ancient site of the destroyed Jewish Temple, and, as Muslims believe, the place from where Mohammed ascended to heaven. *Opposite:* The Dome of the Rock is elaborately decorated with marble, mosaics, and glazed tiles. The dome was originally of solid gold, but was later replaced with a dome of gilded lead.

The bridge of land connecting Africa and Asia is steeped in rich, yet tumultuous history. A narrow strip of hills and valleys between the Mediterranean Sea and the vast emptiness of the Arabian Desert, it is insignificant in size, no larger than the state of New Hampshire. And yet no region in the world has played a more profound and eventful role in the chronicle of mankind. No other place has seen so much human drama of such epic contrasts— spirituality and bloodshed, wisdom and intolerance, sacrilege and sacrifice.

The greatest empires of the past have all come to this region: ancient Egyptians, Romans, Greeks, Babylonians, Ottomans, and the Crusaders and colonists of Europe. They each in turn conquered the land, destroyed its cities, and subjugated or exiled its people. But each great conquering power eventually crumbled and disappeared, while an indigenous empire of the spirit— the world's three great monotheistic religions—born without armies or swords, would thrive and affect the course of human events in the centuries to come.

This page: Worshippers at the Wailing Wall press written prayers into its cracks. The wall is the only remnant in Old Jerusalem of the destroyed Jewish Temple. Followers of the Jewish faith stand at the wall and pray; many speak out loud and rock rhythmically.

This page: At the Wailing Wall a Jewish boy has his *bar mitzvah*, a ceremony celebrating his reaching the age of religious responsibility. A boy carries the ceremonial Torah, the book of Jewish law. Portions of the Torah are read daily by Orthodox Jews.

The most beautiful landmark in the Mt. Zion area of Jerusalem is the twentieth-century Benedictine Dormition Abbey with its rounded church and high clock tower. *Below, left:* A modern staircase runs between the ancient walls of Jerusalem's Old City following the Via Dolorosa, or Way of the Cross, enter Jerusalem's Old City through the Lion's Gate (also known as St. Stephen's Gate) at the eastern wall.

Near the Jaffa Gate in the Old City is the Citadel, the restored palace of Herod the Great, originally built in the first century B.C. *Below:* Schoolchildren swarm through the Jaffa Gate as Jerusalemites have done since it was built in 1538.

For the modern traveler, the Holy Land is surely among the most fascinating and rewarding of destinations. Its long, dramatic history has touched every corner of the region, and as the "Land of the Bible" and the cradle of Judaism, Christianity, and Islam, it is the repository of countless historic landmarks and religious sites. Other places in the world—Rome, Athens, Egypt—offer the remains of their past glories and the temples and shrines of ancient faiths, but only in the Holy Land is the distant past alive in the present, not only in worship but in its laws and language, and even in its dress. The modern world has come to the Holy Land, to be sure: Luxury hotels now tower over Old Testament scenery, and newspapers headline the latest political developments in the Middle East. But the visitor will find much that is timeless and unchanged, from the serene holy places to the desert's shifting sands to the noisy bazaars and marketplaces of the world's oldest living communities. It is not difficult for the traveler with a sense of history and a little imagination to experience the sights and sounds of this historic region as it existed in the times of Moses and Jesus and Mohammed.

The History of the Holy Land

The region of the Holy Land, comprising parts of the modern nations of Israel, Jordan, Lebanon, and Egypt, figured significantly in human history long before the writing of the first books of the Bible. The civilizations of the Bronze Age (3000 B.C.) inhabited the world's first cities—Jericho and Hazor—and invented the first practical alphabet and writing system. Known as the Land of Canaan, this was a busy trading route for the Near East and North Africa.

Around 1900 B.C., Semitic nomads called Hebrews, or Israelites, came to Canaan from Mesopotamia. The Hebrews, following Abraham, practiced monotheism—the worship of a single deity. Forced from Canaan by famine and warring armies, the Israelites lived in slavery in Egypt until the time of Moses at the end of the fourteenth century B.C. Moses' leadership, and his cry, "Let my people go," brought freedom and 40 years of wandering in the desert before resettlement in the Land of Canaan. The next few centuries were marked by warfare.

This page, top to bottom: The Church of the Holy Sepulcher is venerated by Christians as the site of the crucifixion, burial, and resurrection of Jesus. On Easter Sunday in Jerusalem, Christians celebrate the resurrection of Jesus Christ with numerous festivities and processions. The Stone of Anointing in the Church of the Holy Sepulcher marks the spot where, it is said, the body of Jesus was annointed before burial. *Opposite:* The vast Church of the Holy Sepulcher was originally built by the Byzantines in the fourth century. After the church's destruction by the Muslims, the European Crusaders restored it in the twelfth century.

In the Old City of Jerusalem, visitors can follow the Via Dolorosa (Way of Sorrows), the tragic path believed to have been taken by Jesus to his crucifixion. *Left:* For this young shepherd in the ancient city of Jerusalem, much of life is as it was in the time of the Bible. *Opposite:* Each year, thousands of pilgrims retrace the last steps of Jesus on the Via Dolorosa. The route is marked with the 14 Stations of the Cross, commemorating various occurrences on the journey to the crucifixion site at Golgotha (also known as Calvary). *Following pages, left:* Tourists entering the mysterious and colorful Muslim Quarter of Old Jerusalem are greeted by a crush of shops, cafes, and bazaars. Bargaining is a way of life here. *Right:* Shopping is an adventure in the *souk,* a shopping area of narrow lanes and alleys in Jerusalem's old walled city. Fine pottery, handmade clothing, antique rugs, and a variety of camel-skin leather goods are among the merchandise on display in the marketplace.

The threat of their greatest enemy, the Philistines, led the 12 tribes of Israel to unite under a single king, Saul. Saul and three of his sons were killed in battle, but his successor, David, expanded the kingdom, taking biblical Jerusalem as its capital. To Jerusalem, David brought the ark of the covenant, the chest containing the tablets inscribed with the Ten Commandments, making the city a religious as well as a political center. The empire of Israel now reached from the banks of the Euphrates to the southern port of Aqaba.

David was followed by King Solomon, whose expansive reign burdened his people with heavy taxation but produced the first temple for the worship of God, on Mt. Moriah in Jerusalem. Upon Solomon's death in 922 B.C., the kingdom split in two: The northern tribes formed a new Kingdom of Israel under Jeroboam, with its capital at Shechem, and the southern tribes retained Jerusalem as capital of the Kingdom of Judah, ruled by Solomon's son, Rehoboam. The word *Jew,* derived from Judah, would come to be used for all Hebrews.

This page, top to bottom: The busiest of the entrances (and the most ornate) to the Old City of Jerusalem is the Damascus Gate. The many churches found in Jerusalem's Old City reveal how important religion is in this region. The El Aqsa Mosque is Israel's largest mosque and, with its gray dome, is actually the fourth structure built on its site; the earlier ones were damaged by earthquakes. *Opposite:* Between the Dome of the Rock and the El Aqsa Mosque is a fountain, where Muslims remove their shoes and wash their feet before standing on holy ground.

From the vantage point of an ancient Jewish cemetery on the Mount of Olives are seen the Dome of the Rock and the crowded cityscape of Jerusalem. *Below:* At the foot of the Mount of Olives is the Russian Church of Mary Magdalene and the Church of All Nations.

There followed a period of invasions and conquests, first by the Assyrians and then by the Babylonians. The Babylonians, led by Nebuchadnezzar, destroyed the temple in Jerusalem and enslaved the leaders of Judah. In the fifth century B.C., the Persians under Cyrus allowed the Jewish exiles to return to Judah and rebuild the temple and their holy capital. From the year 333 B.C., remnants of Alexander the Great's Greek conquerors ruled the Middle East. When the Hellenist rulers, the Seleucids, prohibited all Jewish religious rites, the Jews, under the leadership of the Maccabeans, revolted. Their victory led to the reestablishment of the Kingdom of Judah, which thrived until the arrival of troops of the Roman Empire in 63 B.C. For the next six centuries, these lands, renamed Judea and Samaria, were territories of Rome.

A man born in the Judean town of Bethlehem, during the early years of the Roman occupation, would become one of the most revered and influential people who ever lived. The Christian religion is based on the life and teachings of this man, Jesus. A carpenter in Nazareth for most of his life, Jesus did not begin his ministry until he was about 30 years old.

This page, top to bottom: The Church of All Nations, also known as the Basilica of Agony, is the site of the Garden of Gethsemane, where Jesus was arrested the night before his crucifixion. Numerous religious structures are in the area of Gethsemane and the Mount of Olives, including the Tomb of Mary. In the garden of Gethsemane, gnarled olive trees have existed since before the time of Jesus.

Preceding page: With its onion-top domes, the 100-year-old Church of Mary Magdalene at Gethsemane is recognizably the work of Russian Catholics. It is also among the most beautiful of Jerusalem's churches. *This page, above:* The City of David is the 3,000-year-old section of Jerusalem once ruled by King David and his son Solomon. *Right:* This area is the site of extensive archaeological excavations, the ancient past being recovered slowly and with great care. *Following page:* Diggers work on an excavation site at the City of David in Jerusalem. Throughout the Holy Land, archaeologists and volunteers are working to uncover remnants of the region's ancient past. Some sites date back to the Paleolithic era.

In Jerusalem and its outskirts, excavators have uncovered elaborate tombs from the Old Testament era. They were largely the resting places of anonymous wealthy Jerusalemites but were often named after figures from the Bible. These tombs, cut directly from blocks of stone, are the pyramid-topped Zachariah's Tomb (top), Tomb of Yeheshabat (bottom, left), and Tomb of Bnei Hezir (bottom, right).

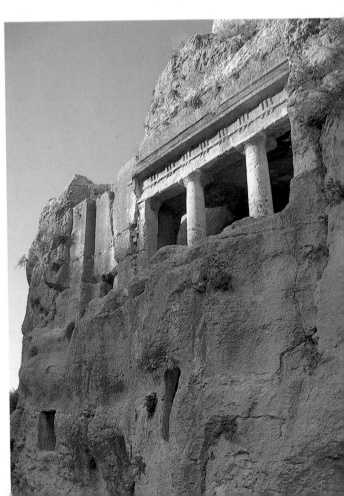

The holy city of Jerusalem contains shrines and churches representing the full spectrum of Christian sects, from Roman Catholic to Greek Orthodox to Coptic. The impressive Russian Cathedral of the Holy Trinity looks more like a castle than a church.

At the Israel Museum in Jerusalem, the remarkable Dead Sea Scrolls are uniquely displayed in a structure called the Shrine of the Book. *Below:* The Shrine of the Book was designed to resemble the lids of the clay jars in which the oldest known copy of the Old Testament was found.

According to Christian tradition, Jesus took his mission—to announce the coming of God's kingdom, and to show God's love and mercy—to the region around Galilee. Capernaum, near the Sea of Galilee, was his headquarters. Of his many disciples, Jesus chose 12 men to assist him, and they became known as the apostles.

As Jesus' influence grew, and he came to be seen by many as the *Christ* (the Messiah prophesied in the Old Testament), he was perceived as a threat to the Judean powers. The Romans feared his popularity would provoke a revolution, and the Jewish leaders believed that a Roman backlash would destroy the Jewish nation.

In Jerusalem, in the garden of Gethsemane, on the slope of the Mount of Olives, Jesus was arrested and questioned, first by the Jewish leaders and then by Pontius Pilate, the Roman governor of Judea. Jesus was charged with treason, condemned to death by Pilate, and crucified between the crosses of two thieves on an outlying hill called Golgotha (also known as Calvary).

In 1947, in one of these caves near the ancient community of Qumran in Israel, a young Bedouin discovered the first of the Dead Sea Scrolls, beautifully preserved manuscripts of the Bible nearly 2,000 years old. *Below:* At Qumran are the ancient ruins of the Essenes, members of a second-century Jewish sect and the authors of the Dead Sea Scrolls.

The years after Jesus' crucifixion saw both the spread of Christianity and numerous Jewish revolts against the Roman rulers. In response to these rebellions, the Romans destroyed the second temple at Jerusalem, and following the Bar Cochba revolt in 135 A.D., much of biblical Jerusalem was leveled and replaced by a new Roman city named Aelia Capitolina. By 330 A.D., pagan Rome had itself become Christian, with Roman Emperor Constantine as ruler of an empire that encompassed southeast Europe and southwest Asia. This period, the Byzantine era, brought renewed glory to the Holy Land: The Church of the Nativity in Bethlehem and the Church of the Holy Sepulcher in Jerusalem are among the many fine religious structures built during this period.

The Byzantine era ended with the spread of Islam. The third of the three great religions to come out of this part of the world, Islam was founded by Mohammed (A.D. 570–632), who was regarded by Muslims as the last and greatest of a line of God's prophets, which included Abraham and Jesus Christ.

Preceding page: A spectacular view of the harsh and arid region of Israel's Dead Sea. This inhospitable landscape has been the scene of some of the most dramatic incidents in the history of the Holy Land, including the last stand of the Jews against the Romans at Masada and the destruction of the biblical city of Sodom. *This page, top to bottom:* Near the presumed site of the doomed city of Sodom on the Dead Sea are large rock salt formations. The southern tip of the Dead Sea is a bleak and uninhabited stretch of salty water and sand. The Dead Sea, more than 1,300 feet below sea level, has eight times the amount of salt found in most sea water.

Tourists explore the ruins of the fortress and palace of Herod the Great, Masada, built in the first century B.C. This desert retreat was intended as a safe haven for Herod in case of an attack by Cleopatra's armies or an internal revolt.

The spectacular fortified plateau at Masada is where a band of Jewish rebels temporarily held off the Roman army (A.D. 73), before committing mass suicide. The fortress appears to blend with its mountainous surroundings.

This page: A remnant of a wall in Herod's vast complex at Masada. In the palace, carved out of the rock, some of the 2,000-year-old interior
s very well preserved. The ruins at Masada remained hidden and unvisited until major excavations began in the 1960's.

Preceding page: In Israel's eastern Negev desert is an extensive excavation of the ancient town of Tel Arad, dating from the time of the Kingdom of Judah. *This page:* Tel Beer Sheva is the excavated site of biblical Beersheba, once the southern outpost of the Land of Canaan. *Below:* In the parched Negev, a Bedouin shepherd tends his herd—an image unchanged over the course of 20 centuries.

Mohammed was believed to have received revelations from Allah, the Muslim's true and only god. His sayings were recorded in the holy book of Islam, the Koran. It is believed by Muslims that Mohammed made his ascent to heaven from the Temple Mount in Jerusalem.

In A.D. 638, Muslim armies under one of Mohammed's successors, Caliph Umar I, conquered the Holy Land. They took control of Jerusalem, considered by Muslims to be the third holiest city after Mecca (Mohammed's birthplace) and Medina (site of Mohammed's tomb).

At the beginning of the eleventh century, Caliph al-Hakim commanded the destruction of the original Church of the Holy Sepulcher and many Christians became victims of persecution. In retaliation, Pope Urban II called from Rome for a crusade to wrest control of the Holy Land from the Muslims, and the Crusaders captured Jerusalem in 1099. For a time, both Jews and Muslims were forbidden to live in the Holy City. But the European knights' hold on the region was tenuous, and there were five more crusades over the next few centuries.

Just off the main north-south highway going toward Sinai are the ancient remains of Shivta. The city was built by the Nabataeans, an ancient Arab people, and further developed by the Byzantines. *Opposite:* On a hilltop in the heart of the Negev are the ancient ruins of Avdat. The city was created by the Nabataeans in the third century B.C. to service passing spice caravans. Most of the remaining structures, however, were built in the Roman and Byzantine periods.

On the stark Coral Island near Eilat, Israel, are the ruins of a granite fortress built by the Crusaders. *Below:* Until recently, visitors were not allowed to tour Coral Island, which is in Egyptian territory.

A modern Egyptian flag flies above the ancient site of the Grey Crusader castle on Pharaon Island. Pharaon Island, in the Gulf of Aqaba, was one of the most isolated outposts of the twelfth-century Crusaders.

Although the Crusaders did not maintain control of the Holy Land, they built numerous fine churches and spectacular fortresses during their stay.

The Ottoman (Turkish) Empire began its rise in the fourteenth century, with the Ottoman Sultan Selim I gaining control of the Holy Land in 1516; the Turks would administer the area until World War I. In 1917, the British General Allenby led a victorious invasion of Jerusalem, and Arab troops led by the legendary T.E. Lawrence (Lawrence of Arabia) fought the Turks in Palestine, Syria, and Transjordan.

After World War I, the League of Nations mandated the British to rule Palestine. The Jews, who had left this region in the *diaspora* (dispersal) after the revolts against the Romans, began returning to their Promised Land in great numbers throughout the 1920's and 1930's. Jews and Arabs came into repeated conflict as the former worked toward creating their own Jewish state.

This page: In the desert wastes of Sinai, the tribes of Israel wandered for 40 years following their exodus from Egypt. Mt. Sinai is considered the approximate spot where Moses received the Ten Commandments. One of the best-preserved ancient sites in the Sinai is the monastery of St. Catherine. *Opposite:* Visitors who make the arduous trek to St. Catherine's Monastery, in the wilderness of the Sinai, will find rare art works dating from the early Christian era.

In the years following World War II, the European colonial powers determined borders and gave independence to several Middle Eastern territories, including Jordan and Syria. The quandary of the British Mandate in Palestine was resolved by the United Nations, which established, in 1948, the State of Israel. As a result, the surrounding Arab countries immediately declared war, but were unable to defeat the new Israeli nation. Since then, military encounters have been frequent, most disastrously—for the Arab side—in the Six Day War of 1967. In less than a week of fighting, Israel's neighboring enemies lost great stretches of territory, including the Gaza Strip, the Golan Heights, the West Bank, and East Jerusalem.

Today, it is a bitter irony that this ancient land, considered holy by so much of the world, remains the focus of so much conflict.

This page: On the shores of the Mediterranean are the remains of Caesaria, the once-grand creation of Herod the Great. It was named in honor of Herod's patron in Rome, the emperor Augustus Caesar. One of the most impressive archaeological sites in the Holy Land, Caesaria's remaining structures include a huge Greek-styled amphitheatre (center) and the beachside aqueduct (bottom). *Opposite:* Near Haifa, Israel, is the site of the ancient Jewish city of Bet She'arim, where an elaborate necropolis (city of the dead) was found in caves on a hillside. The large chambers and coffins, however, had long ago been looted by grave robbers.

A Journey Through the Holy Land

The natural starting point for a journey through the Holy Land is Jerusalem, the City of Gold, once considered the center of the world. It has existed for over 5,000 years.

From modern Jerusalem, visitors pass through the Jaffa Gate into the old walled city. With its narrow, crowded streets, cacophony of tongues, kaleidoscope of colors, and the age-old tangs of spices, incense, and fresh-baked bread, it is little changed since the era of the Bible; only the tinny blare of portable radios and the camera-toting tourists betray that it is the twentieth century. Past the *souk* (open-air bazaar) and the old Jewish quarter is the Temple Mount and the site of the Second Temple of Judaism. The Western Wall, also known as the Wailing Wall, is the place where Jews come to pray. It is the only remnant of the Second Temple complex. In the place where the Alter of Sacrifice of the Jewish Temple once stood is the golden Dome of the Rock, one of the holiest shrines in the Islamic religion. The beautiful building is 1,300 years old and almost perfectly preserved. At the southern end of the platform is the eighth-century El Aqsa Mosque.

The Holy Land is home to a fourth, lesser-known religion, Bahaism, a modern religion that stresses universal brotherhood and equality. It is centered in the port city of Haifa, where Bahais have erected a number of impressive buildings, including the Universal House of Justice.

The beautiful port city of Haifa and the blue Mediterranean beyond; the green-roofed Archives Building of the Bahais dominates the foreground. *Below:* Haifa climbs from the sandy beaches of the Mediterranean onto the green, wooded slopes of Mt. Carmel.

Above, left to right: Mirza Husayn Ali, the prophet and Promised One according to the Bahai faith, is buried at his home in Bahji, near Ac Israel; his tomb is the holiest shrine of the Bahai. The huge Mosque of Ahmed el-Jazzar in Acre houses a cherished relic: a hair from the beard of the prophet Mohammed. *Below:* Throughout the twelfth century, Acre was a stronghold of the Crusaders, as is evident in the remains of many of its buildings.

Preceding page: In northeastern Lebanon, the magnificent and unique ruins of Baalbek are renowned for their Greco-Roman temples and shrines to older gods. The exact origins of the city are lost to antiquity. *This page:* The second-century Temple of Jupiter at Baalbek, built by the Roman Emperor Antoninus Pius, was considered one of the greatest wonders of the world. *Opposite:* Baalbek has been visited and admired by travelers for many centuries. Although an earthquake in 1759 took a great toll on the ruins, the enormous acropolis remained and recent excavations have uncovered several more buildings, adding to the splendor and size of the city. The acropolis' great pillars and pale gold stones can be seen for miles.

Above: Today a sprawling town of 50,000 residents, ancient Nazareth was the small village where Jesus lived for 30 years. *Below, left to right:* The Church of the Annunciation in Nazareth, Israel is built on the traditional site where, it is said, Mary experienced the visitation of the Angel Gabriel. The Church of the Wedding Feast at Cana commemorates the site where some believe Jesus performed his first miracle, turning water into wine at a wedding.

Above, left to right: Tourists visit the Franciscan Church on Mt. Tabor in Israel, the site of the transfiguration of Jesus. The ancient city of Megiddo is at least 5,000 years old and was an important military center for King Solomon. *Below:* The *tel* (archaeological mound) at Megiddo shows evidence of more than 25 levels of different settlements.

The luxuriant hills near Tiberius descend to Israel's Sea of Galilee—actually a lake. *Below:* A serene glimpse of Galilee, where Jesus "calmed the stormy sea" and walked on water.

From here one can follow the final footsteps of Jesus on the Via Dolorosa—the Way of Sorrows. Each year, thousands of people trace this most tragic path in Christian religious history—the route Jesus took to his crucifixion. The Stations of the Cross, which commemorate incidents along the way, are indicated by semi-circular cobblestones. The Via Dolorosa leads on to the Church of the Holy Sepulcher, believed to be the site of the crucifixion and burial of Jesus.

Bethlehem, the birthplace of Jesus, is a short distance south of Jerusalem. The "little town" of old is now a large and thriving township. Bethlehem's Church of the Nativity is built on the site traditionally believed to be the manger where Jesus was born. Northeast of Jerusalem on the West Bank (controlled by Israel since the 1967 war) is Jericho, an oasis city with more than 100 thousand years of history. No archaeological remains have been found of the wall that "tumbled down" in the fabled attacked led by Joshua, but the area encompasses numerous historic monasteries and synagogues, and the fabled Spring of Elisha. South of Jericho, along

This page, top to bottom: The ruins of Capernaum, headquarters of Jesus' ministry in the Galilee, include an early synagogue, a large basalt church, and the house of Jesus' apostle, Peter. One of the most awe-inspiring archaeological sites in the Holy Land is the large *tel* of Hazor, an international capital in the fourteenth century B.C. In the Upper Galilee, the ruins at Bar'am include one of the best-preserved synagogues of early Israel.

Modern Jericho, an oasis eight miles north of the Dead Sea, lies near the remains of the oldest known city in history, also called Jericho. *Left:* At the site of biblical Samaria, visitors can walk along the columned streets dating from the city's Roman period.

the Dead Sea, is Qumran. In one of the many caves there a Bedouin smuggler found an ancient jar containing the first of the Dead Sea Scrolls, intact manuscripts that give an incomparable glimpse into life in biblical times.

Farther south, beside the viscous waters of the Dead Sea, is Masada and the awesome palace-fortress of Herod the Great. A cable car takes visitors to the mountaintop site, where fierce Jewish zealots fought their bloody last stand against the Romans. Beyond, in the desert wastes of the Negev, are Mt. Sinai and the ruins of numerous Byzantine churches, and the ancient ports of Aqaba and Eilat. This desert was once ruled by the mysterious robber kingdom of the Nabateans, and their capital, Petra, is the most unusual and spectacular ancient ruin in the world: Its massive buildings were carved directly from the rose-red mountainsides.

To visit the land where Jesus first taught the ideas of the New Testament, one must leave the desert for the lush greenery of Galilee. Nazareth, where Jesus grew up, boasts the large Church of the Annunciation, built on the site where the Virgin Mary is believed to have met the angel Gabriel, and the Church of St. Joseph, built where the Holy Family once lived. Capernaum,

This page, top to bottom: Jesus' birthplace, the "little town of Bethlehem," is now a sizable Arab township. The Church of the Nativity in Bethlehem, Israel, is built on what is believed to be the exact spot of Jesus' birth. Christian pilgrims come from all over the world to Bethlehem's Basilica and Manger Square.

The terraced fields outside Bethlehem look much as they did when Mary and Joseph arrived in the town just before the birth of Jesus.

High in the Judean Mountains, Hebron is the burial place of the Patriarchs, a site venerated by Jews, Muslims, and Christians. *Below:* The Cave of Machpela in Hebron is, according to the Bible, the burial site of Abraham, Sarah, Isaac, and Jacob.

on the Sea of Galilee, was Jesus' headquarters for the three years of his ministry in the area. It was here that he preached, pronounced his disciples "fishers of men," and, according to the Bible, performed miracles. Excavations in Capernaum have turned up the remains of the actual house of Jesus' apostle, Peter.

The nearby Tiberius Hot Springs, with its naturally heated, therapeutic mineral waters, has been a health spa since Old Testament days—legend has it that King Solomon created the springs with a magic spell. South of the Sea of Galilee—actually a lake—one can follow the quietly flowing River Jordan. It was in this river, near Jericho, that Jesus was baptized by John the Baptist.

The Mediterranean region is filled with numerous remnants of past invaders. Ancient Caesaria was once a territorial capital of Rome, and its archaeological sites are among the most impressive in the Holy Land. Many buildings and relics of the era of the Crusades are on view in the port of Acre. The Knights of the Cross, under Richard the Lionhearted, made Acre the capital of the Latin Kingdom, as it was known then, until the city was

conquered by the Islamic Mamelukes in 1291. Farther north, in Lebanon, are the legendary Roman ruins of Baalbek, with the stunning Temple of Jupiter and towering columns of rare marble.

The visitor to the Holy Land—pilgrim, archaeologist, or tourist—would need many months to explore every site of historical or religious significance. Still, there is no other part of the world where so much of human history is concentrated on so small a piece of land. In a single day of touring it is possible to see the landmarks of an amazing spectrum of world events, from the first stirrings of civilization, through the rise and fall of conquering empires and the spread of the great religions, to the conflicts that capture today's headlines. The modern traveler to the Holy Land must, of course, contend not only with a rich, complex itinerary but also with the volatile geopolitics of the Middle East. Regardless of current events, however, the ancient ruins, holy places, and the drama, passion, and spirit of this region will surely continue to stir and inspire all who visit.

This page: In a wilderness of mountain and sand, 100 miles south of the Dead Sea in what is now Jordan, lies the fascinating lost city of Petra. Once the capital of the mysterious Nabataean community, Petra's huge buildings and tombs were carved directly from the rose-red rock. Among the awesome ruins are the 200-foot royal mausoleum, an immense theater, and the silk tomb cut out of the cliff face.

The Arab village of Um Qeis in northern Jordan is the site of the biblical Gadara. *Right:* The Greek Orthodox Church of St. George at Madaba, Jordan, is home to the famous sixth-century mosaic map of the Holy Land. *Overleaf:* On the colonnaded streets of Jerash, Jordan, an ancient Roman trading center, one can still see the marks of chariot wheels made some 2,000 years ago.

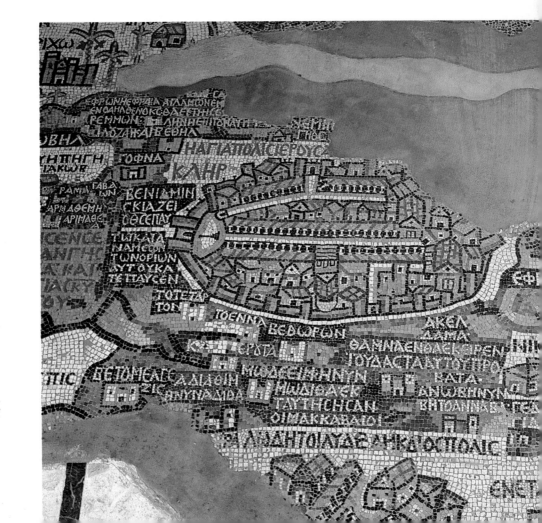

Index of Photography

All photographs courtesy of The Image Bank except where indicated *.